MW00649538

PORTALS:
A Memoir in Verse

To Kathy,
for poetry.

PORTALS:
A Memoir in Verse

Poems by

Nancy Owen Nelson

Nancy Owen Nelson
5/17/21

© 2019 Nancy Owen Nelson. All rights reserved.
This material may not be reproduced in any form,
published, reprinted, recorded, performed,
broadcast, rewritten or redistributed without
the explicit permission of Nancy Owen Nelson.
All such actions are strictly prohibited by law.

Cover design: Shay Culligan
Cover photograph: Danny Rebb

ISBN: 978-1-950462-09-4

Kelsay Books Inc.

kelsaybooks.com
502 S 1040 E
A119
American Fork, Utah
84003

A long time ago, I walked through one of those portals, one of those doors that have always seemed to lead me to understanding.

Bruce Weigl, *The Circle of Hanh: A Memoir*

~~~

Come across the rainbow bridge to Asgard, where the Norse gods live!

Rachel Piercy, "To Asgard!"
from *Falling out of the Sky: Poems About Myths and Monsters*

About the Poems

Portals: A Memoir in Verse follows the narrator as she enters the doorway of a portal to experience images from her dreams—imagined, historical, familial—which impact the narrator's consciousness during sleep and meditation. In some sense in these poems, she enters Asgard, the mythical Nordic kingdom within Yggdrasil, the tree which supports the universe. As they explore world of dreams, these poems often "time travel" to connect history with the present.

Acknowledgments

The poet gratefully acknowledges the editors of the following journals and books in which these poems were published:

Grosse Pointe Congregational Church Arts Ministry, 2018. Call and Response 2: Poets and Artists in Dialogue: "Beckett Living on Rue des Favorites in Paris: December 1948," and "At the Matrix Theater, Mexican Town." An earlier version of "Beckett" was inspired by artist Jackie Rybinski's painting, Hold On.

South Dakota Review: "On Finding *Lord Grizzly* in Hemingway's Library"

The MacGuffin: "Hair"

Weathered Voices Online Journal: "Blood Fountain"

Lyceum: The Fine Arts and Literary Journal: "Walking the Line with Johnny Cash"

Graffiti Rag: "Heat, Night, and Dusty Roads"

Roll: A Collection of Personal: "Fertility," in an essay, "Fertility"

Ardent Writers Press, "Poplar Ridge," in *Searching for Nannie B: Connecting Three Generations of Southern Women*

Oberon Poetry Magazine: "Yggdrasil"

Contents

Small Matters: Three Scenes

On a wet Michigan afternoon walk
she slows her pace to watch
a lone leaf like a small vessel,
spiral from a high branch,
dance to the sidewalk below. All
others have fallen. This one
alone has waited—a holding on.

After a brief rain in Arizona mountains
when bleached bones of animals
are shiny with moisture,
an alpine squirrel, tiny striped body,
pointed nose and ears perked, steals
a drink of water from a flowerpot.
He does not steal the solitary pansy.

In Texas, a young woman, newly married,
lies asleep next to her husband,
her face toward his, their hands
clasped in gentle communion. As yet,
they have no children. They trust
the future, though it will bring them
no more than a lone leaf,
a drink of water, a solitary pansy
left to bloom alone. It will bring
them only the wisdom of holding on,
the power of small matters.

You Scaly Monster of the Amazon Captured in a Black Lagoon for Science

after a film by Guillermo Del Toro

1.

My eleven-year-old eyes
watched your rough-hewn body
as it swam, looped over and under
the weeds and plants, watching her
as she looped under and over.

You thought she was a fish woman,
your true mate.

You were in love, and so was I.
You captured her, took her to your
den, while I sighed for you, and
like her, knew you meant no wrong,
wanted only her for your heart.

You disappeared into the depths,
bullets riddling your trunk,
never to be seen again.

Forever alone.

2.

Creature with a soul longs
for love. He sees her, mute
woman, does not know her
flaw, feels only passion.

From her heart, she gives him
eggs, kisses, music, dance.
His scaly body becomes
beautiful when dancing with
*You'll Never Know How Much
I Love You.*
No longer mute,
she sings the song
just one time.

They think he is a god,
he heals her wounds,
he heals himself.
He takes her away
into a distant den,
the shape of water.

He is with her forever.

And forever I will dream.

Beckett Living on Rue des Favorites, in Paris, December 1948

after paintings by Caspar David Friedrich and Jackie Rybinski

He stares at the wallpaper, leafy green vines
curl about themselves as his mind loops round
an image of two men contemplating the moon,
half uprooted tree branches like claws, like the
curling vines on the wall. "Hold on," he tells the actor
on the other end of the phone, and he exits the room,
receiver resting on the desk, annoyed that his quiet
was disturbed by the phone's jangled ringing.
His chest cough rattles as if the Turkish cigarettes
so renowned for their flavor have blasted a channel,
a road, into his lungs despite the *pleasant,*
delicate aroma . . . sweet, mild, fresh flavor.

He shuffles back to the phone, looks for his glasses,
looks for what he was thinking about, what words
he wanted to type when the phone cut into his
consciousness, his thought. What was it?
He cannot tell the actor playing Vladimir
that not even black English breakfast tea
will serve to give him clarity.
He cannot tell the other actor, the one playing Estragon,
who sits by his desk waiting for the call to end,
what he himself is doing or thinking,
how, in the misty night of his brain he sees only
despair and fools waiting by a tree.

There is No Third Act, and Godot Does Nothing

I read about this mysterious chap
in French class, fall of 1966,
was just engaged, ripe for discontent,
disillusion, wondering why I
needed someone so desperately,
looking for meaning in a phrase
or a glance from anyone with
special knowledge, an explanation
of being. *a personal god with white*
beard quaquaquaqua outside time
without extension who . . . loves
us dearly with exceptions for reasons
unknown but time will tell...

At the end of Act Two I searched
for another page, another act or
scene to make sense of what
was not there. I thought my copy
was defective, just as I was,
without a clear path, without
a goal, without a savior.

Minute after minute I waited
with two men by a tree,
in the moonlight.

What does he do, Mr. Godot?
Vladimir asks the Boy. *He*
does nothing, the Boy says.

There is no third act.

On Finding *Lord Grizzly* in Hemingway's Library

In a land denied by America
Hemingway's house in
San Francisco de Paulo
holds in its heart his ways,
his dusty books—nine hundred,
I'm told. His hands touched
each one, opened, savored it,
placed it in a hallowed spot
among the others.

A random photo taken
by a friend, her love of books
urging her, unknowing,
to move her hand, to aim,
record the moment. She
forgets her gesture. But
later, her random act
brings back fifty years,
and two American voices
struggling to be heard.

I imagine 1954,
the year Papa won
the prize for peace.
I imagine his hand
closing over this book,
a journey, another voice.
A story of endurance,
of crawling over earth
to avenge desertion.
I imagine him
reading, in this time of
careful peace, the story
once, then again. He

pauses, looks into space
a moment, imagines dirt
and worms, beetles, the
grinding pain of broken leg,
the fury of clawed flesh,
of maggots on the back.
He marvels at the courage.
He could be the man crawling.
He would know
how the land lies,
how to endure the world,
a place where wounds
and pain light the rugged
path over the next hill,
the hiding behind brush
until the predator gives
up the scent. He would
know what to say to the
man, the other voice.

He would recognize a brother.

Patti Smith Sings Dylan at the Nobel Ceremony

October 17, 2017

She's there, tuxedo cuffs in place, long grey hair
hangs straight down her back, frames her face.
Sings about a *hard rain falling,* about wandering,
looking about in the world of pain and beauty,
about protecting a *blue-eyed son* from what
she knows in this harsh world full of sharp edges
and need, of poets dying in gutters, of crying
clowns robbed of threads of dignity, bracing
themselves in alleys and on lonely highways
for the next onslaught of hard rain.

She stops, and with her, the orchestra. She's
forgotten the words. She's frozen. She pauses,
waits, *I'm sorry, I'm so nervous.* But maybe
she's really remembering instead the boys in
camouflage crouching in jungles or rice paddies,
rifles raised, waiting for the moment when one
of them may step on a mine, get blown to
smithereens before he knows what happened.
Maybe she's remembering the naked children
running away from flesh-searing napalm, from
villages where they felt safe, only a short time ago.

So she pauses, she's *sorry,* she says, closes her eyes
and goes on, sings about wounds of love and hate,
about poisoned water (does she think of Flint?)
and tries to understand, to express, a world
where black is the color and none is the number.
Where a hard rain will always fall no matter
what we do about it.

Handel's Silence

in memory of Linda Cain

Winter darkness enters a sanctuary
swelling with people. Seeps
through the door closed,
then opened, sounds
muffled for sanctity.

Grandfolks, parents,
children, young women
and men move slowly
down aisles that slant
toward a creche,
center of adoration.
Children whisper, giggle.
Parents caution,

Shhhh. Keep quiet.
The music begins soon.

Poinsettias
against candlelight
cast shadows on walls,
they are ghostly flickers
on spiraled ceilings.

This old church,
1920's Methodist
Brownstone,
is a place for sinners,
for hope in coming
of Christ tide.

In this small town,
in this old church,

quiet waits to burst
into sound.

Our little choir,
Our imperfect voices—
some will saw and grind,
others will quiver, catch
in mid-note.

Even these sounds will
bring whispers,
even the children's,
into silence.

We enter, sibilant
swishing of black robes,
red satin hoods, soft click
of heels on wooden steps.
We climb into the loft.
It will hold our voices
like a cradle.

Messiah,
masterpiece of rhythm.

Out of silence we begin.
*And the glory, the glory of the Lord
shall be revealed, shall be revealed.*

We mount our chorus,
climb to ecstasy,
reach the peak.
We fly, quiver at the top,
then stop, cut notes off,
lips and teeth bite a phrase,
close it.

The final chorus comes.
We remember our director's words:
Altos, come in on the half beat.
Sopranos, wait for the entry.
You will hear basses stop.
Remember, when we reach
that peak, that place
where we pause only a second
before a last cry of joy,
a hallelujah of victory . . .
remember the silence,
the power of no sound,
crescendo.
cry of passion.

Quiet. A cough.
The floor creaks beneath
shifting weight on worn pews.
A moment passes.
Silence ends.

The ultimate cry of triumph,
Hallelujah! Hallelujah!
fills the church,
raises faces up, toward
swirling spirits,
toward shadows in rafters,
the cry kisses notes that blend,
then soften
into blessed quiet.

We cannot speak,
released from sorrow,
we can only sing.

Stille Nacht

Christmas Eve, 1818
From Oberdorf Austria, chords of your peace
will ring through decades, hopes of silent night
free from battle, from grisly death,
end of Napoleon's wars. A simple song
about quiet, about a holy birth, words scratched
hastily on a tablet, music which longs to stop
the fighting, if for just one night.
Only one night.

Christmas Eve, 1914
100,000 troops make short truce,
sing the hymn about quiet and peace, pass
a bottle, kick a soccer ball, even bury the
dead left lying untended for much too long.
For that one night, they rebel. They will not
fight the battles of the powerful. Instead,
they will, for only one holy night, cease,
be quiet, in the knowledge that peace
comes only when we lay down our weapons,
when we do not forget
that war is
an invention
of humankind
not of God.

Christmas Eve, 2018
Tonight, at least, we lay aside our anguish
at wars that rage around us. We sing
of this night, a silent and holy night,
of peace, of hope.
We turn our faces away from darkness.
We turn toward emerging light.

Portals

after a photograph by Danny Rebb

Day bleeds into night,
door sways open as
pigeons squawk above,
land on crumbled concrete,
shattered glass. Roots of
weeds and grasses emerge
from mud and slime.

The arch beckons, leads
toward passages beyond the
ragged door, a Venus-like
key painted on the side,
as if this door is an entrance
into mysteries of Woman, as
if it is a portal into
hidden, dark truths.

Beyond, colors of carnival—
scarlet, or aqua, burnt yellow—
an arch as if to an arena
welcomes, *Cross the rainbow
bridge. Come into Asgard,
into your world of dreams—
houses with attics full of
treasures—ragged dolls,
letters on onion skin paper,
brittle to the touch, tattered
lace. Rooms where you feed
your mother and your son,
where you see into a mirror
not darkly, but face to face,
the legions of those who
came before, centuries*

28

of kin wrapped in war,
basements where you fear
to go for what you might see there.

Here you must feel again choking grief,
a gold necklace around your
neck from a loved one who
took his life after giving this
gift. Go where you see him
always following you,
always claiming his place
with you. Where you can
no longer deny him, where
if you do, he will die again.

Venus with Mirror: on Mars' Close Encounter with Earth

August 2003

I'm waiting for him tonight.
The sages say he will come
closer to earth than it is possible
to imagine. Thousands of years
since he has been so very
near. Thousands more before
he returns to my realm
of influence.

It seems longer,
millennia even, since we
transcended the heavens
together. Eons since we were
as one being, two sides of
the same coin, two parts of
a whole, yin and yang.
Forever since we pledged
to tame our excesses, work
together, find a common
balance between his war,
and my love, a place to dispel
the horror of bomb blasts
and human torment, flesh
rent apart, families
losing the threads of kin
and fearing them buried
in unmarked graves.

Love and war. Why could
we not make it happen, a
universe in which the excess
of one is tempered by that of
other?

I await him. My breathing
is shallow, my heart pounds
against the breast he once
fondled and kissed, once
pledged his eternal faith
to protect. But now instead,
he turns toward Earth, that
planet of confusion, where
killing and war and power
are at home. Why does he
seek her as his lover, when
I await him?

I must move behind the sun.
I must wait yet more long,
long millennia, before I meet
my love, ready with my
mirror to show him what he
has become.

On a Bleak Winter Afternoon, a Day Sprinkled with Snow and Soot of War

in anticipation of the invasion of Iraq, 2003

I am an ordinary woman
beyond childbearing,
beyond affecting the future
my son faces, a future of menace
and pain, blood for oil and power.
No voice of peace is heard,
not mine, nor my son's, nor the
voices of the sons and daughters
who perch on the edge—the precipice—
of adulthood. Their lives, all
of our lives are the playthings of
power. We hold *no* truths to
be self-evident. No words in winds
of hope to soothe us, no spring breezes
replace the dark and filthy
bellows of power and war.

My Sister Whose Middle Name was Chandler

I want to tell you about my sister,
who, before I came home from the hospital,
dressed like the adult she was not, wore
heels and a suit, and went
to see me, a baby in a maternity ward,
broke the rules in Madigan Hospital,
on an Army base in Washington State.

And how, when I was just one year old,
I'm told, she came home from school and scooped
me up into her arms, changed my diapers, read
me stories. How she played with me on a blanket
under an oak tree, across from West Lafayette
High School, the echoes of band and football
practice in the distance. How she walked her fingers
up my arm, playing *Creep Mouse,* walked them
up to my shoulders, my neck, until
my giggles rose above the blaring band
instruments, the football crunches and grunts.

And how her heart was broken
by a lieutenant in Alaska, Harry, a man
whose dark eyes and wavy hair must have
reminded her of our father, whose hair was
now mostly gone, but whose eyes still held
the glimmer of a young man. How when
Harry went home to the States, he vanished.
And how she brooded and whimpered softly
in her bedroom.

And I want to tell you how, when I went to sleep
after losing a tooth, she tiptoed into my room
to leave a quarter under my pillow, how
she drew little fairy footprints leading up to the
pillow, to the edge where the coin lay
waiting for me to find it.

I want to tell you how she married a man she promised
to obey. And how, as her babies came, she was
less and less herself, less and less the tomboy who,
when the guys in an Alabama town saw her walking
toward home base, yelled "Chandler's at the bat!"
as if she were Babe Ruth. And how she hit the ball up
and over the fence and they were never prepared
for that swing. But how her prettiness won
her suitors who wanted to marry her,
how that beauty faded.

And how she left me.

And how she left herself then too.

I want to tell you how, over her last years, her steps slowed,
and her vision doubled, and how, at fifty,
her children grown and out of the house, her husband left,
and how, after that, she was alone.

And I want to tell you that when we buried her,
she wore a blue negligee, her favorite color,
and she clasped fresh roses
in her unmoving hands.

My Mother's Clothes

are soft.
fold easily after washing,
house her frame, 93 years old,
a body pushed pulled
twisted changed through time
toward an ending
she cannot foresee.

My mother's clothes
are stained with food dropped
forgetfully from a dinner plate
that holds more than she can eat,
food that tantalizes her with memories
of salty ham, fresh tomatoes
from a garden on a hot afternoon
in Alabama, June of 1918.

My mother's clothes
are pulled this and that way
by arthritic hands. She fumbles
for pants and shirts, fumbles as she
pulls them on because her eyes
cannot help her with habits
of a lifetime.

My mother's clothes
are beautiful.
Like her, they are very much alive
with colors of spring flowers—purple,
or blue, or pink, or yellow—or deep
richness of autumn—brown and orange.
She sits in her chair like a queen
newly crowned, sits as straight
as her spine will allow.

She looks into space before her.
She relives, I'm sure, moments
when her body was straight and beautiful,
her clothes were not stained not twisted,

like the clothes she wears in her dreams.

Bath Powder

Tonight, after a hot bath
with bubbles floating
on the steaming water,
I pat off my body, rub down
my skin with lotion.

I pick up your bath powder,
a round, yellow plastic box.
Jean Naté, scent of clean,
fresh mother smell.

This mitt once touched your skin.
Even when you were old,
you cared about cleanliness,
broke all rules about
ancient women who forget that
once they were young and lovely.

Even near the end, you still
found beauty in a day, ambers or
rusts or browns of falling leaves
or in the taste of chocolate
pudding eaten *before,* not after
chicken or ham steak and peas.

You awoke every day to say
you valued life. Even the night
you died you never gave up on living.
I rushed to you from an airplane,
feared I would not be there at the end.
You quipped in those last moments
that you would like to join me
in a toast to your life,
with gin and tonic.

In this simple box of powder,
your sweetness remains
the soft mitt, a silent reminder
that you are close to me,
captured even now
in my ritual of bath.

Wringer Washer

It had to be a Maytag, 1950,
Lafayette, Indiana. I was four.
A white monster in the kitchen
churned water, spewed, cranked.
I worried my tiny fingers would
be crushed in the wringers or
catch, disappear in this grinding thing
that gleamed when afternoon light
came through the kitchen window.

In the daytime Dad was at college.
ROTC uniforms filled our house
at night. Young men visited
my sisters, laughter, piano,
Mom playing jazzy tunes, *Kitten
on the Keys,* or sad love tunes,
When I Grow Too Old to Dream,
or *Indian Love Song.*

My throat was full. I could not sing,
choked out words instead. Wanted
to hide in case Dad came in again
bare-chested, lipstick marks around
his nipples. *I have tits too,* he said
one night and the room was really
quiet. Wonder if Mom washes
lipstick off his clothes? Wonder
if the white monster does a good job
of washing away sadness?

Soda Fountain: 1950

for Sue Petricca

cup against my lips, thick, smooth,
feels like marble on my tongue,
early morning coffee time.

white marble like the countertop
of countless soda fountains in small
towns across America—stops in midst
of summer heat and traffic. *I want a drink
of Coke or RC Cola. How can Mommy
drink coffee in this heat?* I put my cola
bottle against my sweating forehead,
wondering whether I dare ask for
a chocolate malt, made with that handsome
blender–ice cream and chocolate
milk and malt powder?

or maybe a Horse's Neck, a tall fountain
glass filled with vanilla ice cream, ginger
ale poured to the top, the foaming of
the ale and ice cream making a cool,
white neck?

I wait, my drink warming in my wet
hand, longing for a hamburger and fries
from that cook whose once-white shirt
is spotted with grease. *Delaney's burgers—
the best in town* the sign says over the grill.

Hey fella, says Daddy. *How about some
of your fine burgers? Onions and catsup
and mustard, and some fries too. Make it
three.* We wait, my mom, my dad, and I,
sitting at the soda fountain, the smooth
marble of the countertop, with threaded lines
of dark across the beige surface.

Ironing

1954

The day is hot and humid.
This Alabama summer afternoon
makes me sweat, taste the salty
water as if rolls down my face
into my mouth, drips off my chin.

Big Mama, or her maid Mandy,
spray each blouse and skirt,
each pair of pants with water,
roll in a towel, set aside to wait
until the steam iron lays its smooth
heat on each leg, or arm, or breast
of clothing. Iron touches cloth.
Vapor rises past my face. I breathe deep
again, fan myself, and smell
fragrance of burning heat,
of clean, starched goods.

Hair

Sit down. Let's talk about your hair, Faye tells me
as I enter the salon on a cold Saturday afternoon.
*You want highlights? It's time we did them again,
one more time, or two. After that, we're done.*

I sigh and say, *Yes, you are the expert. Your craft
is your art.* She replies, *I am a work of art.*
We laugh as she lifts my hair, a few strands at a time,
onto strips of aluminum foil. I ask her, *Tell me a story.
Me?* she asks. *I don't have stories. All I know is
hair, hair, hair.*

But I remember otherwise. I remember the stories
she's already told me, about Lebanon, her homeland.
About coming here in '74 when as a young woman,
she loved the rare sight of snow, how she walked in it
in high heels despite the risk. How when she returned
months later, homesick, returned to find her
homeland in flames, how, trapped there,
she no longer wanted to stay in the land of exploding
cars and human flesh baked onto windows and doors.

*Here some people say we don't need government. I'll
show them no government. I'll show them Lebanon,
with scant electricity and water, with no support for
the poor. I'll show them what it's really like with
no help from anywhere. I think of this when I hear
of the bans, the cries of "terrorist" about my people.
Where am I supposed to go? Certainly not home
to that burning place of blood and skin.*

Signs of Weakness

after a song by Simon and Garfunkel

You tell me that I am too scattered,
that I should *slow down, you move
too fast* as Simon and Garfunkel say.
If I did change the way I live my life,
not moving on four or five levels at once,
not hearing ideas and connecting them
to others like a family tree whose branches
seem to be twisted and tangled but lead
to meaning—student comments about war,
a new wisdom learned from Islam,
the way my cats greeted me this morning,
sandpaper tongues on my cheek,
an indiscriminate and juicy sneeze from
the alpha cat, Thelma, all over the bed clothes,
the way the pansies on the back
deck look after the sudden drop below freezing
last night–perky, standing purple, pink and yellow
as if not frozen but calling Spring into action.
If in some way I did not pull all these together
with my migrant childhood as an Army kid,
then I would never know the lush moments
of clarity, the vision that comes with
knowing, as the Native Americans do,
the "we are all related." I would not know
percolating cells, particles of the quantum
universe, constant movement into a maelstrom—
all would not end up in this beautiful
pink and gold sunset.

Blood Fountain

There is a fountain filled with blood
drawn from Emmanuel's veins.
and sinners washed beneath that flood
lose all their guilty stains.
                    William Cowper, ca. 1772

I.

A church in
North Alabama
September 15, 1963

In the paltry hot sanctuary
flies buzzed and old men snored.
We sang of the crucifixion
sin and repentance.
Women and little children,
men with bellies popping from
their shirt fronts walked to the altar.
They cried, tears crawling down cheeks
like so many rivulets in a spring
of feeling. As the flies buzzed
we wept in joy, thought of
blood fountain,
promise of salvation.

But we knew that we lied.
When we looked in each other's eyes
we saw shame.

II.

Sixteenth Street Baptist Church
Birmingham, Alabama
September 15, 1963

Down the road apiece,
in a little church
in a big city,
they cried and wailed their sins.
They saw the blood fountain
on that morning
with the little girls lost
their hopes gone,
their dream un-resurrected,
no salvation.
They wept their rivulets of fear
while we sat piously
waiting for them to come to our door,
waiting to shut them out.

Walking the Line with Johnny Cash

A hot, humid day near Houston,
driving along a beach white
with sizzling sand. The back seat
of Uncle Prentiss's car is hot enough
to cook an egg, much less my
ten-year-old flesh. *I keep a close watch*
on this heart of mine, a guy on the radio
sings. Cousins Sally and Patsy
and a neighborhood girl,
we are *all* there in the car with tall
Daddy Prentiss, whose long legs stick up
above the accelerator, knobby knees
reaching upward toward his chest.
He can't *ever* sit still. His nervous
fingers diddle on the steering wheel,
the dash and the seat beside him.
Windows down, humid air blows
in my face, a headache like
sickness above my eyes, aching pouches
press in, turn my tummy to acid.

The radio keeps blaring that song
about walking the line, about somebody
who couldn't quite trust himself
to do the right thing
with the right person
at the right time.

A promise to be true, a tie that binds,
a voice sounding *so* hillbilly
that I don't want to hear it, don't want
to like it, don't want to admit it.
I'm enchanted by a regular beat and a voice
that's steady. He talks about simple

things and love, about life and mistakes
and challenges, and about forgiveness,
all to a rhythm that sounds like
the steady beat of big truck tires
on the highway.

After all, I *am* just ten years old.
All I know about life is that grownups
always seem to know what they are doing
all the time. But this song, this voice,
this man, here he is singing about being
uncertain, about making mistakes.

On the way home, Uncle Prentiss
stops at a gas station, goes inside to buy
a cold six-pack of Lone Star, long-neck
bottles sweating in the cardboard container.
He pulls out the first 100-dollar bill I've
ever laid eyes on, flashes it quick and crisp
at the guy pumping his gas.
Prentiss gives us some bills,
lets us buy those pop-up popsicles, the ones
you push up through a tube to lick the
red and white and blue sherbet inside. The
cool ice soothes my mouth. The radio plays
that song again, the one about trying to live right,
about making mistakes. Prentiss rolls up
the car windows, turns on the air conditioner
and we start home.

Hey Mr. Cash, you sure know how to
make that guitar sing!

My headache is gone.
I close my eyes and listen
to the steady rhythm of big truck tires
on the highway.

She, Herself

an early October 1963 memory

Taxicab with rusting fenders, driver with hard face,
intent on pacing himself in the night's traffic,
passes quickly on my right,
whips around car after car, left and right,
barely missing fenders already bumped, scraped
upon other cars scraped, bumped, left to rust
on winter's salted roadways.

And she recalls how
                she, herself,
torn between fascination of the driver's hair
parted on the left, falling in greasy strands to his shoulders,
and where he was taking her in the black night,
turning and twisting in the darkened streets,

how
                she, herself
sat on the back seat—torn plastic,
the tear cut sharp into her bare thighs,
caressed them with protruding cotton stuffing,

how
                she, herself
sat with muscles taut,
legs drawn tightly together as if remembering
her father's warning about what nice boys didn't do,
and wondered if the driver with greasy hair
would take her where she didn't want to go
but where she had to.

Would that she had stayed,
                              she herself,
in that Greyhound Bus station
in Birmingham, Alabama,
stayed to pace the room
loud with squalling babies,
cluttered with dirty old men.
They were not yet ousted for loitering,
they sat or lay upon soiled seats.

Hours she had paced in that waiting room
watching the eyes watching her,
                              she herself,
as in and out of the restroom she went,
clutching her purse to her boyish chest,
clasp on the inside, held tightly against
her beating breast.

She gazed over her shoulder,
remembered stories of violence ˙
in streets of that dark city only weeks ago,
of bombs in churches and little girls
surprised in their Sunday best.

And waited for someone who never came.

Instead she found herself,
                              she herself,
cast about wildly in the back seat of this taxicab,
clutching the sticky door handle with trembling fingers,
breathing stale smoke of the last rider,

being taken to Aunt Pearl
(Mama gave her the phone number.
She didn't even know her),
to a darkened house,
to a room smelling of mothballs,
to a fruit and marshmallow salad.

Heat, Night, and Dusty Roads

Not much to do in our little town
but talk about the boys and
sneak by their houses after dark
in cars with bent fenders
and listen by their windows
hopin' to hear a voice say
the most ordinary things,
like *turn up the tv* and *shut up
Billy Joe, I'm tryin' to watch Elliot Ness
on the Untouchables*

or sit in our bedrooms with the lights out
waitin' for one of them to drive by on
the dirt road that swirled with hot dust
only a few hours ago, watchin' for headlights
and listenin' for the groaning of an old engine

and while we wait we talk about our bodies
and how they change and how we treat them
and how we feel and how strange it all is

or talk about the party where we danced
up close with sweaty palms and cheeks
to the sounds of the Platters or *Soldier boy,
oh, my little soldier boy I'll be true to you*

and what happened afterward and who drove home
with who and how it is that it ended up different
from the way it began.

Not much to do in our little town it seems
so delicious thinking of the hot, sticky
nights full of promise and pain.

Golden Boys

to Joni Mitchell

I was *a free man in Paris,* twenty-three,
with a permanent groove in the record of my brain,
walking the Champs Elyseé alone. I carried
dull pain down that broad avenue,
thinking that somehow, I was making history,
in the city of the guillotine, sidewalk wet
under my feet, cafes ringing in my ears.

I met a god-like man with flaxen hair,

a student of international studies, Georgetown,
traveling in Paris alone, like me,
a woman who just lost her lover.
On the Seine, taking in the sights
on shore from our boat, he leaned back
into the slanting rays of sun,
his golden hair shimmering light.
His hair belonged in the Rodin Museum,
where we strolled by an uncast monument of Balzac,
and in the garden, the Gates of Hell.
We paused at *The Thinker.*
I went home to my hotel room alone.

No explaining a wounded heart.

A year later, home in Birmingham, Alabama,
I drank beer while another golden boy
grilled steak on his patio. I listened to your
song, Joni, about you and your pain, your rebellion,
strolling down that same avenue,

about *dreamers and telephone
screamers*. And after that bright afternoon,
never would I hear your song again without
thinking of golden boys, and of the day when,
along the Champs-Elyseé,

I thought I was free.

There Was the Book

my lover brought to me, in a women's ward
of St. Vincent's Hospital. The book he gave me
before he walked away into the shadowed hallway.

Nuns tended me, looked kindly into my tired face.
Perhaps they knew nothing about the baby.
Perhaps they knew nothing about the father.

There were moments of stolen delight.
There was the church, Anglican, as
Catholic as you can get without being Roman.
There was the defrocked priest who put his hand
down my dress, squeezed my breast
as he tried to persuade me not to leave my husband
for the lover, and there was the other priest
who told us we had to decide.

There was the wife.
She and he sat next to me in the church choir.
After I lost the baby, she told me not to kneel,
to take care of myself.

She knew it was his.

And there was the book of Saint John of the Cross.
I'm told he suffered dark nights without God.
It was a small, gilt-bound volume,
holy, full of anguish.

Clipping Hedges

Electric grinding interrupts the chatter of neighbors.
A baby girl babbles on her mother's lap while
next door he clips the hedges, hates the minutes he has
to spend measuring lengths, plying the town's standards
on lush green foliage. *They cannot block the house.*
Cannot jut clumsily from perfectly grown, hybrid roots.
Community standards, neatness, symmetry.

He longs for granite mountain, ground soil,
nitrogen leaking subtly into spindly bushes, junipers
and pines. He longs for unevenness, asymmetry.
Jagged rocks, jaunt of a vagrant elk
as it climbs the hill behind his new home, a lizard
as it scuttles swiftly and silently up the side of the house
or across the yard. He longs for sunrise half-blocked
by rain clouds bringing monsoons, droppings of birds
on the deck.

He finds a spider in the hedges, large and black, body
of a check pattern, yellow and black, bright yellow
stripes. Suddenly he knows he has cut the web
with errant clippers. The spider remains, rigid against
the house, waits to rebuild its lair. He leaves it
to its work, remembers the granite mountain and the elk
and the lizard, the sunrise hidden behind clouds,
the bird droppings. Remembers how much he hates
the grinding of the clippers,
how much he loves the wild.

My Husband Is a Liberal at Heart

He hides his politics in silence.
He's an engineer, and after all, engineers
are supposed to be
rational
left-brained
balanced
organized.

How can such a person be a liberal?

He drives a big truck and plays golf for
sport. He does all the cooking, and he
will care for a pet as if it were his child.
When we put down our cat Butterscotch,
he cried alongside me, remembering how
she came down into his basement workroom
to keep him company while he chiseled and
ground away at metal and wood.

He thinks of others' feelings, finding a way
to soothe a friend's pain, or to call me on
my cell phone after a minor argument to
tell me he loves me *whatever happens.*

He nurtured my aging mother when I
was at work. Took her for rides in her
wheelchair on the short path around her
nursing home, gathering leaves in the
fall, or hearing her say, *This is the forest
primeval* about all the green growth
around her. She asked every single time,
Where is that from? Though he didn't

remember Longfellow's *Evangeline* (he's
an engineer after all), he behaved
as if it was a new question, discussing the
possibilities of authorship.

He painted my mother's fingernails,
asking her if she wanted summer pink,
or a fall deep orange/red, like the leaves they
gathered. I can see him now, sitting with his
large body bent over her bed tray,
working with her splitting nails, cleaning
the fungus under each one,
filing, cutting, painting, until Bee was the
envy of the nursing home. *Her son even
paints her nails,* they said.

After she died, I promised never to forget
these things, especially the fingernails, or
his gentleness, sitting with her to listen
to *The Great Gatsby* on audio, or bringing
poetry with music tapes to her room to
play and listen.

My husband is at heart a liberal. In his
silence, he played my mother's music
at her deathbed. In his quiet, he checked
her pulse, put his large, rough hands
before her face and nodded.

Poplar Ridge: Bethel Cemetery, New Hope, Alabama

to my grandmother, Nannie B Russell Chandler

Once your voice rose
above the others,
sang shape notes
whole and lovely,
filled that old church.
Now you are silent,
the only sounds cicada
and a distant car engine.

Has anyone visited
since your daughter,
a ten-year-old wondering
why her mother died?
She lived a life
shaped by your absence.

This girl is gone,
her life a vessel half-filled,
heart never healed from
a place you left open, raw.

Only when she sang
or played, her fingers
running up and down
the keys like yours,
did anyone remember
to speak of you.

And only years later.

Did others come to mourn?
A baby from your body.
Here you were,
then you were gone.

Moss grows over
stalwart stone,
letters worn
corrugated like marble.
106 years ago
you were buried here.

Fertility

Burr Oak Street in rural Michigan
glows with brown, gold,
yellow, orange leaves.

October 9. Pains begin at 12:05 a. m.
A cool night, bracing itself
for colder nights to come.

I know the signs, count the seconds
between each throb, electric
belly currents.

I climb steps to the first floor slowly,
one at a time, brace myself,
grip iron railings,
for each wave is

like a heartbeat
like a tribal drum
like an urgent call.

Outside, wet wind blows leaves
against the house. It's
almost Halloween.

***

At three years old I am a ghost
in white sheet, eyes peering
through ragged slits.

I moan, and my girl voice rises
through an Indiana fall night,
joins wet winds

bearing down on leaves, mostly yellow,
some orange, a damp carpet
on lawns, sidewalks.

This will be a long night of monitors,
ice chips, moans, counted breaths,
dampened forehead patted dry.

At 8:11 a. m. he will emerge,
his cries like a chicken clucking.

I will take him home. By then,
trees will stand barren of leaves.

Road Trips

I remember the restaurants
along the highway, from Detroit

to Alabama, the times I took you inside Denny's
along I-70–you a baby then, and just the two of us,

you perched on my left hip,
white-blonde hair curled around your face,

and neck—the hair of angels.
You dined on cottage cheese, crackers—

grown-up fare for such a little boy—but left piles
of cracker crumbs under your chair, trails

that Hansel and Gretel could follow.
When you smiled your teeth shone, uneven,

later straightened by braces.
When you cried, you would free no one

from your discontent. You cried on, even when (I thought)
your needs were met, when you were dry and fed.

I never wanted you to weep as a grown man,
weep for home, wander about with no crumb

trails to follow,
nothing lacking.

King Kong, My Mother, and a Bridge in D. C.

In a dream last night,
I was driving through
Washington D. C.,
capital of our great nation.
Driving over a bridge
to find a way home.

Mom, who is dead now,
was asleep in the seat
next to me. A huge gorilla
loomed in the sky above us.

Where are we? I asked aloud.
This was not New York City,
nor was the giant monkey
atop the Empire. He was floating
toward the road,
his gigantism blocking
sun and clouds.
One gargantuan foot
lowered to the bridge,
hominoid claws
clutching the concrete
just ahead,
the other poised,
ready to crush the side
of our car.

I kept driving.
Mom was still sleep.

I tried hard to stay awake.
Mom, help me out here.
I'm trying to get through
this. I need your help.

She never woke up.
We never made it
between the giant legs.

New York Memory

Spring 1992

It seems much longer ago
than only last july
when we walked through
those streets skin cloyed
with ripened air and
tainted sounds and the
puerto rican woman starring
at nothing on broadway
while we passed the
urine-drenched grate
and the man in rags
called out *Gimme another drink!*
or yet another in an alley,
F... you, I want my car!

In this cool Michigan end-
of-winter-early-spring,
for a gasping moment
sweltering choked sounds
of taxis and ambulance
return, mingling old glamour
with new fear—a man selling
papers called the two of us
Charley's Angels.
Where's the third one?

The stench of horse dung
and beer and rotten fruit rinds
in garbage mingled
above the glittering lights
of XXX films and girls for

cheap and hawkers, children
dragged away by the hand of
their older brother from the circus
and into a dark alley where waits
who knows what—
maybe a knife?

Or a taxi rear-ended into
Nicole's Tearoom
window at 1:00 a. m.

Or maybe the next
day a lovely breakfast
over fruit cups and coffee
with white table linen
and Nicole's window patched
with rough wood panels
and the forgotten frenzy of
a night in july on broadway.

Last Day's

to my sister, Betty

Were you knitting up the raveled sleeve of your cares,
those days when I watched you breathe in and out,
in and out, beset with tubes, chords, machines, tracking
your life pattern? The rest of us stood by,
watching your shadow blanch.

Did you know we were there? Sister, son and grandson,
niece, nephew, friends? I sang *Summertime* the way
I sang it years ago, my baby babbling in the background,
you and husband John playing soft guitar.
I sang *You are My Sunshine.* You taught me
that song, must have heard me repeat the lines,
When I awoke dear, I was mistaken.
I did not hang my head and cry, then, but instead
crooned *Row, Row, Row Your Boat,* my version
at three, *Life is butter dream.*
Did you smile inside, remembering?

I held your hand, felt a gentle stirring of fingers.
You turned your face slightly toward me.

Soon memories smoothed out a wrinkled past:
There were no alarms, no beeping, no pain, no loss,

only peace,
the end of this day's night.

My Sister Reads *Jane Eyre*

I found a milk dud in my slipper
this morning, a flattened, sticky pad
of chocolate and caramel,
my favorite.

Two days ago, my sister died. Had I called her
six days ago, she and I would have belly-laughed
at the absurdity of it all.

The absurdity of it all.

My sister was reading Jane's story, wondering aloud
"How can people treat a child like that?" when Jane
was locked in the Red Room.

Betty never finished Jane's story, never walked with
her through the love of Rochester, his betrayal on Jane's
wedding day, her desperate journey through the wilds
in the cold and wet.

*In the last days, Betty could not walk across the room
from her bed to breakfast, could not make coffee.*

My sister will never know how Jane, when offered marriage
without love, walked into wilderness on her own,
returned to find her true love blinded by a fire,
his crazy wife killed when she jumped from a balcony
after setting the blaze.

*Instead, Betty's true love died in a car, on a
lonely mountain road in Arizona.*

She will never know how Jane made it,
how she cured her man.

Betty's man is dead, she found another man,
but only for a while, guitars strumming together,
duet lasting only so long.

My sister will never know how, in the end,
Jane prevailed.

And how, in the end, she did not.

Steaming Concrete: 1986

In spring, I am a rose's thorn.
I leave safety, colorful
streets with florid gardens,
leave for speechless love,
damaged brain, aphasia.

This dark summer bears no fruit,
no roses where he and my son
dribble basketballs again and again.
Their bounce, a hollow heavy heart,
pounds on steaming concrete.

In eight years, he will cut his wrists,
drain his body overnight.
Rigor mortis in the morning.

But today, in 1986,
he brings me a rose.
Though cut too soon,
its petals are soft, fragrant.
Only one frees itself, falls,
as he places the flower
in my hand.

At the Matrix Theater, Mexican Town: Her Eyes Unmoving, See Nothing

They do not blink. They are crystalline pools
looking beyond even the weeping
of her darker partner, the man who
moans over and over,
Stay with me sweetie.

After she talks with a young woman,
You're one of my kids, I hear her say,
this large woman climbs toward a seat,
misses a step, a backward fall, full force,
her shaved head striking concrete floor,
a cracking sound.

She lies there still, the moans
of her lover rising and falling
like waves, like chords of a love
song, like a wizard's incantations
to turn back the clock only seconds,
erase what I've seen.

We are hoping her ride will arrive,
waiting for her rescue,
for healing men in EMS jackets
to come, to lift her long body,
not yet lifeless, to a stretcher,
her neck brace-bound.

They take their time—ten minutes.

After she is gone, after
the red lights cease,
a play about guns begins.
It's about a southern senator
who grows a pair, speaks
his truth, fights against
unexpected violence,
a high school shooting.

In the very first scene, the senator cries out.

How could I believe in a god
that would let this happen?

Walk-In

Dearborn, Michigan

Saturday morning late,
husband sick with fever, his
nose runs like an undaunted river,
cough echoing in cavernous chest.

We sit among those waiting, whose
names crawl slowly up a digital list—
Smi, D. 1 hour, 20 min., Jo, S.
Children with parents—twin girls
about three years old holding hands,
hijab-covered mother. One girl points
down a long hall. "Let's go there,"
she says, while mother guides both
gently toward reception.

Sweet Home Alabama blares from
a cell phone as a woman in ragged jacket
walks behind a man in a wheelchair,
his partial leg points forward as if
to show the way. She stops, drops
her backpack on the floor, while
where the skies are so blue/Lord,
I'm coming home to you resounds
at full volume until she answers, gives
directions to the second floor, walk-in
clinic. The man rolls toward the desk,
undaunted.

Three hours later, we leave behind
the fifty coughs and sneezes, the women
and men with babies, the blare of
Sweet Home that says so much about
where some folks leave their hearts.

75

Robert E. Lee Reads *The New York Times* at Starbucks

May 2018

He sits with the Op-Ed section, his right ankle
resting on his left knee, a cup of cappuccino
steaming on the table in front of him.

His grizzled beard twitches as he
thinks about his battles, the lost cause
he took up, about all the dead soldiers
on both sides, the dead president.
He reads about shootings in a high school
in Texas, wonders why any young man
of character would do such a deed.

He pauses from his reading, takes a sip
of coffee. The foam coats his mustache
as two dark men come in and sit down.
He thinks nothing of it, thinks instead
of the 1500 Confederate dead
at Pickett's Charge, finishes the last
delicious drop, folds his paper,
walks out into the streets of Lexington,
Virginia.

I'll pray for all the men who fell,
he mumbles to himself, shakes
his silver-grey head as a boy barely misses
him on a skateboard.

There is no great cause to fight for,
he thinks, no honor codes to redress.
Not in this strange new world, this noisy
place everybody seems to talk at the same
time without saying anything at all.

Robert E Lee's Yoga Pipe Dream

What if,

before Appomattox, before Gettysburg,
Robert E Lee had practiced yoga? In a parallel
universe, he could have found that

doing Downward Facing Dog would bring
his world view upside down,
usurp his truth to say that no man should own another,
that stretching his legs and calves against
the earth this way would do better for him
than sitting on Traveller, watching his men die
at the hands of the Yanks.

What if,

before Chancellorsville, his greatest victory,
when he sent his soldiers with doomed
Stonewall Jackson to take the left flank
around the backside of Union General
Hooker, the man who wanted a dictator to win
this bloody war,

what if instead,

Lee did a Sun Salutation, pointing his arms
straight above him, heaven-ward, while he
folded forward, stepped back into a plank,
then lowered himself down on his belly,
humbled to the earth?

What if then Lee pushed himself up on his hands
to Downward Facing Dog again,
stepped forward
into another fold,
humbled himself
toward earth
once more,

if he then slowly, carefully, followed his breath,
raised up to his full height, arms lifted above
hoary head toward heaven,
then lowered his arms through to heart center?

What if,
instead of the glory, the call for courage,
the honor and passion for region,
he chose country and peace,
freedom to enslaved?

Then we would not care about statues,
about words or torches,
signs or marches.

Instead, we would know the prana
of life,
the ongoing of peace.

All Marvelous

I'm going to punch the next man in the nose that gets ugly about you,
wrote Feike Feikema to Henry Miller on March 11, 1944.

1.

All those years ago, when I was Feike, not Fred,
I dreamed of the marvelous, as Henry wrote,
It's *always beautiful. Anything that is marvelous
is beautiful. Indeed, nothing but the marvelous is beautiful.*

Yes, that's what I thought, a young man with wife,
baby on the way, and only one book to my name. Thought Miller
was the cat's meow. Would fight for him, would punch the man
who said he should *lay off the sex, for god's sake.
Women would blanch at your words.*

And he was. The cat's meow, that is. I liked Henry.
Liked how he tapped into the core of the lizard
in people, primal urge, sex, love, babies, working folk,
plowing land, people seen only in Hardy or Steinbeck.

That's what I always wanted, to be like Henry Miller.
I loved women, despite having a wife. But it was all about
being real, understanding human urging. It was what
god put us here for. *It is all marvelous . . . very precious.*

2.

All moments of life are very precious. Fred's right, I think. This
place in me, this pain, I embrace it, like a small cancer that visits
and waits, yearns for an exit, waits until it's cut away
like a rotten tooth, leaving only a gaping hole.

That hole will close, a forgotten crater in the moon,
a *one step* for me away from the notion that life can be free
of *pain and hunger,* that I will somehow be blessed with *life,
not death,* that there will never be an ending to this
compromised, bitter-sweet existence. Like the two tramps,
I will wonder if I'd be *better off alone, me for myself.* And yet,
and yet, I will wait, never alone, I will wait, always
tormented with accursed time. I will wait, for the sweetness
of pain and hunger, for how marvelous, how very precious,
it will all be.

Yggdrasil

after a photograph by Danny Rebb

At first, snow-covered tree, stark against sepia sky,
barn-rust-colored building, *Private Property* on
its side. A second glance of what winter
approximately spreads onto lilies-of-the-valley
scattered below as if falling from the sacred tree,
as if spreading seeds, as if Yggdrasil expands
with noisy, clanging voices, shouts rising
above raucous shouts to be heard.

1.

Sacred arbor, cousin to oak, Druid for door, lore
of ethereal, higher ground. I want to mount the silver
tree, climb up, up through branches until I reach *what?*
Perhaps those Viking blood origins of ancestor,
Rollo, protector of Normandy and of my last name.

2.

I am swallowed up into this tree, in its white erasure.
I hear rude blood voices, silent for all these centuries.
I want to touch my oak, my sign, sister of the ash,
I want to hear, to *be* my wren, bird of singing, bird of soul.
I want to fly to the blue stones of Wales,
sarsen stones pulled, dragged hundreds of miles
to this place of worship.

81

3.

In deep winter,
I see people in red, green, ram's horns, arms lifted
to greet the dawn of shortest day. I want to tell them
that a stream of light will mark the day after
the day of ending darkness, that all will turn
warm with yule log burning and holly branches
to grace the halls and walls of human spirit.

4.

In Midsummer,
The festival of Lithal,
the scent of bale fires drives out evil spirits.
I see Druids in white gowns, men, women,
children with wagons, horses.
With them all, I welcome the flourishing
crops. With them all, I wait for sun as it rises
between ancient stones,
as it brings the longest day.

Notes on Select Poems

"On Finding *Lord Grizzly* in Hemingway's Library." *Lord Grizzly* is Frederick Manfred's novel based on mountain man Hugh Glass' heroic crawl after being mauled by a grizzly bear. The novel was a finalist for the National Book Award in 1954.

"Stille Nacht": The lyrics of "Silent Night" were written by Pastor Joseph Mohr. In 1818, after his transfer the Oberndorf Parish in Salzburg, Austria, he asked musician Franz Xaver Gruber to compose music for his poem. It was sung publicly for the first time on December 24, 1818.

"All Marvelous": Feike Feikema, aka Frederick Manfred, wrote a letter to Henry Miller about the critical response to Miller's "Open Letter" in *The New Republic* about being faithful to his art. Feikema's letter was published in *The Selected Letters of Frederick Manfred: 1932-1954* (University of Nebraska Press, 1988). In this letter, Feikema was addressing Miller's "Open Letter" to James McLaughlin of New Directions, who at the time had failed to publish his books in the U. S. In "Open Letter to Surrealists Everywhere," Miller had praised "the marvelous" in all of life's gritty reality. Frederick Manfred's gravestone reads "It was all marvelous. I don't regret a minute of it, even the pain and hunger were sweet to have. It was life, not death, and all moments of life are very precious." The poem also references Samuel Beckett's *Waiting for Godot.*

***

The inspiration for this collection came from two artists—poet Bruce Weigl and photographer Danny Rebb. Weigl's concept of "portals" to another reality pervades his work. Rebb's urbex photographic interpretation called "Portals" offers a pathway to that other reality. Check out Rebb's work on his fine art Facebook page.
www.facebook.com/Danny-Rebb-Fine-Art-Photography-1238679296276525/

I owe deep thanks to Poet Laureate of the Upper Peninsula of Michigan, Russell Thorburn, for his astute arrangement of the poems and his fine editing; he gave me permission to traverse time, to get out of my comfort zone, and to explore possibilities. Thanks to author Susan Lang for the opportunities she provided me during the Hassayampa Institute for Creative Writing; to poets Angela Gunnell and Olga Klekner for working with some of these poems in our poetry workshop; to poet Dawn McDuffie, whose encouragement and gentle editing helped me to see some of the poems in a new way; to my husband Roger and my son Owen, who inspired me to write poems about them. As always, I give loving thanks to my mother, Nannie B Chandler Nelson, whose love of poetry imbued her life as it does mine.

About the Author

Nancy Owen Nelson teaches at Henry Ford College in Dearborn, Michigan. She has edited and co-edited several academic books including *The Selected Letters of Frederick Manfred: 1932-1954* (with Arthur R. Huseboe) and *Private Voices, Public Lives: Women Speak on the Literary Life.* She has published critical essays in journals such as *The South Dakota Review* and *Western American Literature,* as well as creative nonfiction and poetry in several journals and anthologies. Her memoir, *Searching for Nannie B: Connecting Three Generations of Southern Women,* was published in 2015, and her poetry chapbook, *My Heart Wears No Colors,* was published in 2018.

Follow her at
www.nancyowennelson.com